Featuring:

Tedd Arnold
Joe Berger
Sophie Blackall
Henry Cole
Frank Morrison
Lynn Munsinger
Tao Nyeu
LeUyen Pham
Adam Rex
Peter H. Reynolds
Dan Santat
Judy Schachner
Bob Shea
and Kevin Sherry

MANNERS MASH-UP

A GOOFY GUIDE to GOOD BEHAVIOR

SCHOLASTIC INC.
New York Toronto London Auckland
Sydney Mexico City New Delhi Hong Kong

ISBN 978-0-545-39504-5

Pages 8-9 © 2011 by Bob Shea, Pages 10-11 © 2011 by Lynn Munsinger, Pages 12-13 © 2011 by Henry Cole,
Pages 14-15 © 2011 by LeUyen Pham, Pages 16-17 © 2011 by Peter H. Reynolds, Pages 18-19 © 2011 by Tedd
Arnold, Pages 20-21 © 2011 by Adam Rex, Pages 22-23 © 2011 by Judith Byron Schachner, Pages 24-25 © 2011
by Frank Morrison, Pages 26-27 © 2011 by Sophie Blackall, Pages 28-29 © 2011 by Dan Santat, Pages 30-31
© 2011 by Joe Berger, Pages 32-33 © 2011 by Kevin Sherry, Pages 34-35 © 2011 by Tao Nyeu

12 11 10 9 8 7 6 5 4 3 2 1   11 12 13 14 15 16/0

Printed in Mexico   49

This edition first printing, September 2011

The illustrations in this book are the copyrighted property of the
respective illustrator.
Designed by Jennifer Kelly

Say please!

TURN THE PAGE
* TO FIND: *

Bob Shea on the SCHOOL BUS

Lynn Munsinger in the CAFETERIA

Henry Cole with a STARING PROBLEM

LeUyen Pham on the PLAYGROUND

Peter H. Reynolds in the CLASSROOM

Tedd Arnold on SPORTSMANSHIP

Adam Rex at the DINNER TABLE

Judy Schachner at a BIRTHDAY PARTY

Frank Morrison VISITING RELATIVES

Sophie Blackall at the DOCTOR'S OFFICE

Dan Santat at the THEATER

Joe Berger at the SUPERMARKET

Kevin Sherry at the SWIMMING POOL

Tao Nyeu at a "PICK"-NIC

Don't hog the ball

Wait your turn!

art by LeUyen Pham

No throwing sand in the sandbox

PLAYGROUND MANNERS

Give friends
a boost

Always watch out
for little ones

It's nice to share

Classroom Manners

art by **PETER H. REYNOLDS**

Manners

Help out if you're asked

Don't make a mess

Give a polite greeting

Don't insult the host

Keep your feet off
the furniture

Don't play ball in
the house

art by Dan Santat

HOLD THAT URGE TO MAKE A JOKE ABOUT THE FAT LADY'S SILLY HELMET. TALKING CAN BE DISTRACTING TO OTHERS. (EXCEPT MAYBE YOUR BROTHER.)

STOP KICKING THE SEAT IN FRONT OF YOU! IT'S HARD ENOUGH TO TRY AND ENJOY THE OPERA WITHOUT YOU MAKING IT FEEL JUST LIKE THERE'S A HUGE EARTHQUAKE GOING ON IN THE SEATS.

THERE'S NO FOOD ALLOWED IN THE THEATER! HEY, IT WAS VERY THOUGHTFUL OF YOU TO SHARE, BUT NOT EVERYONE LIKES NACHOS DURING AN OPERA.

HEY, DON'T HECKLE THE PERFORMERS! BE CAREFUL! THERE ARE VIKINGS ON THE STAGE!

art by JOE BERGER

WHAT WAS YOUR GOOFIEST

When I was little, I had a very bad habit of hunching over the table, sticking my elbows out, and waggling them up and down while eating, rather than sitting up straight with my arms down at my sides. My elbows would prod my sister on one side, and my mum or dad on the other. My dad would shout "Wings!" which was my cue to sit up properly and fold my wings down.

Joe Berger's books include:
Bridget Fidget and the Most Perfect Pet!;
Hattie the Bad

It's good manners to have your fly zipped up, right? I had very bad manners for an entire day in the spring of 1985.

© Sonya Sones

Adam Rex's books include:
Frankenstein Makes a Sandwich; *Frankenstein Takes the Cake*;
Guess Again! by Mac Barnett

When I was a kid, I used to draw portraits of the other students. One day, someone asked me to draw the teacher. So I did. A scribble here, a line there, a box for a head, a carrot for a nose, waffle ears, the teacher's name at the top, and just like that I was done. Little did I know, but my teacher was standing there the whole time.

Frank Morrison's books include:
the Keena Ford series by Melissa Thomson;
The Hat That Wore Clara B. by Melanie Turner-Denstaedt;
For the Love of Soccer! by Pelé

I didn't show up to a surprise birthday party for a friend . . . and I was the one giving the party!

Henry Cole's books include:
A Nest for Celeste; *On Meadowview Street*;
Big Chickens series by Leslie Helakoski

Kevin Sherry blows his nose REALLY loudly, like an elephant. He can't help it. On the first day of school, he would blow his nose in front of the whole class. The other kids would laugh, but then realize that was just how he sounded, and wouldn't laugh for the rest of the year.

Kevin Sherry's books include:
I'm the Biggest Thing in the Ocean; *I'm the Best Artist in the Ocean*; *Acorns Everywhere!*

One day at lunchtime I rushed to an art show. I was going to be the judge. I wolfed down a hamburger on the way. At the art gallery I acted like a sophisticated judge of art. I thought I was cool! Later, I found a huge, gross smear of mustardy ketchup on my shirt. Not so cool! Never wolf down your food.

Tedd Arnold's books include:
Hi! Fly Guy; *Green Wilma, Frog in Space*; *Parts*

I once told Santa that the present he gave me at the school Christmas party was stinky. I got a packet of hair bands, when anyone could see I had short hair. My mother made me go to Santa and apologize.

Sophie Blackall's books includ[e]:
the Ivy and Bean series by Annie Barrows;
Big Red Lollipop by Rukhsana Khan;
Wombat Walkabout by Carol Diggory Shields

manners mishap?

UYEN AT WORK
zzzzzzzzz

LeUyen Pham (pronounced "Lay Win Fam") falls asleep everywhere. She is known to fall asleep while other people are talking to her, within the first ten minutes of any movie, when talking for more then twenty minutes on the phone, during any meeting, and once, she nearly fell asleep during a speech that someone else was making about her. Other than that, LeUyen has VERY good manners.

LeUyen Pham's
ks include: *Freckleface Strawberry* by Julianne Moore; *'s Dream* by Archbishop Desmond Tutu; *Big Sister, Little Sister*

I accidentally picked my nose while posing for this portrait!

Tao Nyeu's books include: *Wonder Bear; Bunny Days*

I was on a trip to China. Our group was treated to an elaborate banquet with many courses, including some rather unfamiliar delicacies like jellyfish tentacles. There were a lot of different little bowls set out with sauces. All of a sudden our horrified hosts ran up and pointed out that we Americans were busily dipping our food into the finger bowls. I do remember thinking that that was a rather bland sauce!

Lynn Munsinger's
books include:
Skunks! by David T. Greenberg;
What Sisters Do Best/What Brothers Do Best by Laura Numeroff; *The Underground Gators* by Tina Casey

SLOP

One time there was a dusty western town full of dusty townspeople. Some bad men came and started bossing everyone around.
A mysterious stranger (me!) rode into town and said, "Hey you bad men, stop being so bossy!"
The bad men said, "Why don't you make us?"
"Because I don't make monkeys!" I said.
They knew I was serious, because they got on their horses and bikes and ran away.
As I rode out of town the dusty townspeople looked at my silhouette against the orange sunset and said, "We didn't even get a chance to thank him!"
Which was totally rude of me.

Bob Shea's books include:
Oh, Daddy!; Race you to Bed;
Dinosaur vs. Bedtime

It was my birthday and I could cry if I wanted—which I did every time someone sang the birthday song to me.

Judy Schachner's
books include: *Skippyjon Jones;*
The Grannyman;
Yo, Vikings!

One day I was walking through Harvard Square in Cambridge when a rather cute girl came running at me full tilt, grabbed me, gave me a great big squeezy hug, and then planted a big, sloppy kiss on me. I had NO idea who this girl was! As she pulled back from me and saw my stunned face, she said, "Oh my gosh! Paul said he had a twin brother! I am soooo sorry!!" I politely replied, "Please—don't worry! These things happen," and walked away smiling ear to ear.

PETER H. REYNOLDS

Peter H. Reynolds's
books include: *Huck Runs Amuck!* by Sean Taylor;
Rose's Garden; The North Star

My parents told me that when I was very little (maybe one or two years old), when we were in restaurants I would eat chicken and then throw the bones at the other customers sitting in their seats. True story.

Dan Santat's
books include:
Always Lots of Heinies at the Zoo by Ayun Halliday;
Chicken Dance
by Tammi Sauer;
The Secret Life of Walter Kitty by Barbara Jean Hicks

BURP!